Alfred's
INSTRUMENTAL
PLAY-ALONG

Classic MOVIE
INSTRUMENTAL SOLOS

Arranged by Bill Galliford, Ethan Neuburg and Tod Edmondson

Alfred Cares. Contents printed on 100% recycled paper.

© 2010 Alfred Music Publishing Co., Inc.
All Rights Reserved. Printed in USA.

ISBN-10: 0-7390-7008-8
ISBN-13: 978-0-7390-7008-6

Contents

DING-DONG! THE WITCH IS DEAD

(from *The Wizard of Oz*)

Music by
HAROLD ARLEN

Moderately bright march (♩ = 116)

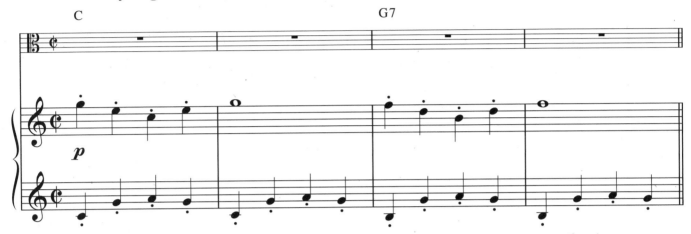

Ding-Dong! The Witch Is Dead - 5 - 1
35128

4

CANTINA BAND

(from *Star Wars Episode IV: A New Hope*)

By
JOHN WILLIAMS

Moderately fast ragtime (♩ = 112)

Cantina Band - 4 - 1
35128

To Coda ⊕

CONCERNING HOBBITS

(from *The Lord of the Rings: The Fellowship of the Ring*)

By
HOWARD SHORE

JAMES BOND THEME

By
MONTY NORMAN

18

James Bond Theme - 4 - 3
35128

James Bond Theme - 4 - 4
35128

GONNA FLY NOW

(Theme from *Rocky*)

By
BILL CONTI, AYN ROBBINS
and CAROL CONNORS

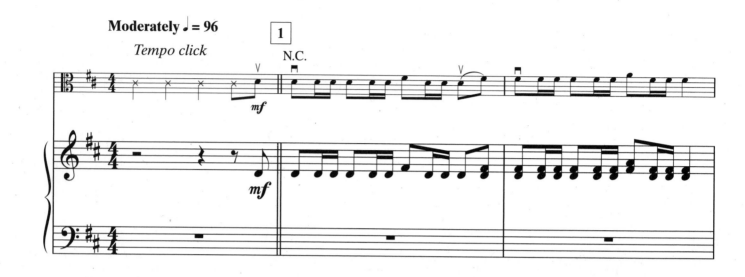

Gonna Fly Now - 4 - 1
35128

RAIDERS MARCH

By
JOHN WILLIAMS

Classic MOVIE INSTRUMENTAL SOLOS

—Contents—

Arranged by Bill Galliford, Ethan Neuburg and Tod Edmondson

 Alfred Cares. Contents printed on 100% recycled paper.

ISBN-10: 0-7390-7008-8
ISBN-13: 978-0-7390-7008-6

DING-DONG! THE WITCH IS DEAD

(from *The Wizard of Oz*)

Track 2: Demo
Track 3: Play Along

Music by
HAROLD ARLEN

Moderately bright march (♩ = 116)

Ding-Dong! The Witch Is Dead - 2 - 1
35128

Track 4: Demo
Track 5: Play Along

CANTINA BAND
(from *Star Wars Episode IV: A New Hope*)

By
JOHN WILLIAMS

Moderately fast ragtime (♩ = 112)

Cantina Band - 2 - 1
35128

Cantina Band - 2 - 2
35128

5

CONCERNING HOBBITS
(from *The Lord of the Rings: The Fellowship of the Ring*)

By
HOWARD SHORE

Track 6: Demo
Track 7: Play Along

JAMES BOND THEME

By
MONTY NORMAN

Track 8: Demo
Track 9: Play Along

© 1962 UNITED ARTISTS MUSIC LTD.
Copyright Renewed by EMI UNART CATALOG, INC.
Exclusive Print Rights Administered by ALFRED MUSIC PUBLISHING CO., INC.
All Rights Reserved

Track 10: Demo
Track 11: Play Along

GONNA FLY NOW
(Theme from *Rocky*)

By
BILL CONTI, AYN ROBBINS
and CAROL CONNORS

Gonna Fly Now - 2 - 1
35128

RAIDERS MARCH

Track 12: Demo
Track 13: Play Along

By
JOHN WILLIAMS

cresc. poco a poco

FAMILY PORTRAIT
(from *Harry Potter and the Sorcerer's Stone*)

By
JOHN WILLIAMS

* An easier 8th-note alternative figure has been provided.

Family Portrait - 2 - 1
35128

Family Portrait - 2 - 2
35128

14

HEDWIG'S THEME

(from *Harry Potter and the Sorcerer's Stone*)

By
JOHN WILLIAMS

*A♯ = B♭.

STAR WARS
(Main Theme)

By
JOHN WILLIAMS

35128

IN DREAMS

(from *The Lord of the Rings: The Fellowship of the Ring*)

Track 20: Demo
Track 21: Play Along

Words and Music by
FRAN WALSH and
HOWARD SHORE

35128

SONG FROM M*A*S*H*

(Suicide Is Painless)

Words and Music by
MIKE ALTMAN and JOHNNY MANDEL

35128

OVER THE RAINBOW

(from *The Wizard of Oz*)

Track 24: Demo
Track 25: Play Along

Music by
HAROLD ARLEN

35128

Classic MOVIE INSTRUMENTAL SOLOS

This book is part of a string series arranged for Violin, Viola, and Cello. The arrangements are completely compatible with each other and can be played together or as solos. Each book features a specially designed piano accompaniment that can be easily played by a teacher or intermediate piano student, as well as a carefully crafted removable part, complete with bowings, articulations and keys well suited for the Level 2-3 player. A fully orchestrated accompaniment CD is also provided. The CD includes a DEMO track of each song, which features a live string performance, followed by a PLAY-ALONG track.

This book is also part of Alfred's Classic Movie Instrumental Solos series written for Flute, Clarinet, Alto Sax, Tenor Sax, Trumpet, Horn in F and Trombone. An orchestrated accompaniment CD is included. A **piano accompaniment** book (optional) is also available. Due to level considerations regarding keys and instrument ranges, the arrangements in the **wind instrument** series are not compatible with those in the **string instrument** series.

Alfred

alfred.com

FAMILY PORTRAIT

(from *Harry Potter and the Sorcerer's Stone*)

By
JOHN WILLIAMS

© 2001 WARNER-BARHAM MUSIC, LLC (BMI)
All Rights Administered by SONGS OF UNIVERSAL, INC. (BMI)
Exclusive Worldwide Print Rights Administered by ALFRED MUSIC PUBLISHING CO., INC.

* An easier 8th-note alternative figure has been provided.

Family Portrait - 5 - 2
35128

30

HEDWIG'S THEME
(from *Harry Potter and the Sorcerer's Stone*)

By
JOHN WILLIAMS

Misterioso (♩ = 160)

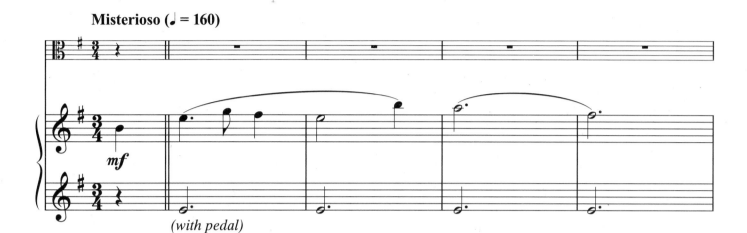

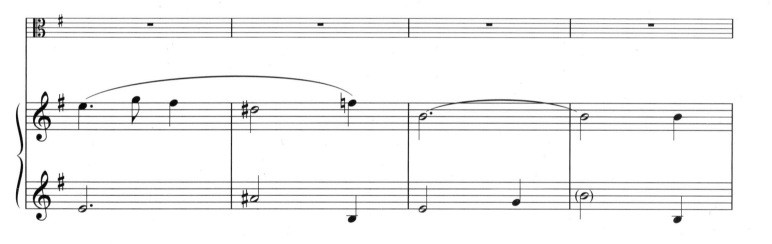

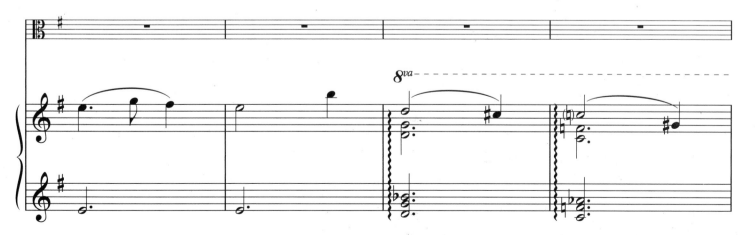

Hedwig's Theme - 5 - 1
35128

34

51 **Bright** (♩ = 80)

55

Hedwig's Theme - 5 - 5
35128

STAR WARS
(Main Theme)

By
JOHN WILLIAMS

Majestically, steady march (♩ = 108)

Star Wars - 5 - 1
35128

40

21

30

Star Wars - 5 - 3
35128

42

IN DREAMS

(from *The Lord of the Rings: The Fellowship of the Ring*)

Words and Music by
FRAN WALSH and
HOWARD SHORE

Moderately slow (♩ = 76)

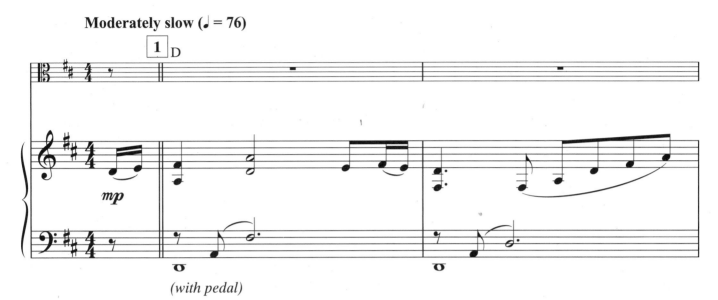

In Dreams - 3 - 1
35128

SONG FROM M*A*S*H*
(Suicide Is Painless)

Words and Music by
MIKE ALTMAN and JOHNNY MANDEL

Song from M*A*S*H* - 3 - 1
35128

48

*Enharmonic chord label (instead of A#13).
Song from M*A*S*H* - 3 - 3
35128

OVER THE RAINBOW

(from *The Wizard of Oz*)

Music by
HAROLD ARLEN

Slowly, with expression (♩ = 88)

Over the Rainbow - 3 - 1
35128

50

Over the Rainbow - 3 - 2
35128

KEEP YOUR STUDENTS PLAYING WITH THESE GREAT PLAY-ALONGS

Arranged for Flute, Clarinet, Alto Saxophone, Tenor Saxophone, Trumpet, Horn in F, Trombone, Piano Accompaniments, Violin*, Viola* and Cello*.

* Piano Accompaniment included

LEVEL 1

Easy Christmas Instrumental Solos
Book & CD

Easy Popular Movie Instrumental Solos
Book & CD

Easy Rock Instrumental Solos
Book & CD

LEVEL 2–3

Classic Movie Instrumental Solos
Book & CD

Harry Potter™ Instrumental Solos (Movies 1–5)
Book & CD

Indiana Jones and the Kingdom of the Crystal Skull Instrumental Solos
Book & CD

Lord of the Rings Instrumental Solos
Book & CD

Selections from Rolling Stone Magazine's 500 Greatest Songs of All Time: Instrumental Solos, Volumes 1 and 2
Book & CD

Star Wars® Instrumental Solos (Movies I–VI)
Book & CD

Top Praise and Worship Instrumental Solos
Book & CD

The Wizard of Oz Instrumental Solos
Book & CD

——— Visit **alfred.com** for more information ———

INSTRUMENTAL ENSEMBLES FOR ALL SERIES

Arr. Michael Story

A versatile, fun series intended for like or mixed instruments to perform in any combination of instruments, regardless of skill level. All books are in score format with each line increasing in difficulty from grade 1 to grade 3–4. Perfect for concerts with family and friends, recitals, auditions, and festivals. Available for brass, woodwinds, strings, and percussion.

Movie Duets for All

Titles: Double Trouble • In Dreams • Singin' in the Rain • The Entertainer • Twistin' the Night Away • We're Off to See the Wizard • Be Our Guest • Fame • Wonka's Welcome Song • Wizard Wheezes • Can You Read My Mind? • Star Wars • Everything I Do • I Don't Want to Miss a Thing • Living in America • Gonna Fly Now • Superman Theme.

Movie Trios for All

Titles: Believe • As Time Goes By • Can't Fight the Moonlight • How the West Was Won (Main Title) • If I Only Had a Brain • Nimbus 2000 • You've Got a Friend in Me • Mamma Mia • Batman Theme • Cantina Band • Imperial March • James Bond Theme • Theme from Ice Castles (Through the Eyes of Love) • You're the One That I Want • Raiders March.

Movie Quartets for All

Titles: Hedwig's Theme • Over the Rainbow • And All That Jazz • The Magnificent Seven • Theme from A Summer Place • Eye of the Tiger • There You'll Be • Blues in the Night • The Pink Panther • You're a Mean One, Mr. Grinch • Parade of Charioteers • Hakuna Matata.